24 Carat Conversations

Rhonda Velez

TRILOGY CHRISTIAN PUBLISHERS

TUSTIN, CA

Trilogy Christian Publishers
A Wholly Owned Subsidary of Trinity Broadcasting Network
2442 Michelle Drive
Tustin, CA 92780
24 Carat Conversations

Rights Department, 2442 Michelle Drive, Tustin, CA 92780.

Trilogy Christian Publishing/TBN and colophon are trademarks of Trinity Broadcasting Network.

Cover design by: Beth Harp Photography, Lagrange, Indiana

For information about special discounts for bulk purchases, please contact Trilogy Christian Publishing.

Trilogy Disclaimer: The views and content expressed in this book are those of the author and may not necessarily reflect the views and doctrine of Trilogy Christian Publishing or the Trinity Broadcasting Network.

Manufactured in the United States of America

10 9 8 7 6 5 4 3 2 1

Library of Congress Cataloging-in-Publication Data is available.

ISBN: 978-1-63769-368-1

E-ISBN: 978-1-63769-369-8

Endorsements

This devotional is an authentic gift, full of grace and freedom. Rhonda has been through so much pain, and she has allowed God to use it for His glory and purpose. This devotional will give you an up-close and personal look into what it is like to have deep faith in Jesus while also learning what it takes to rise above your circumstances. Rhonda has lived a faith-filled life with grace, strength, and bravery, while not letting her circumstances allow her faith to waver. So, get into your comfy chair and in your favorite pjs, and learn how God can bring gold from your trial! This devotional will be just what you need to deepen your faith in a great God who loves you so much!

Julie Scott
Executive Director of Growth
The Unhindered Life

I have had the privilege of knowing Rhonda during the time she was writing this book, and I love how it reflects her own story so honestly and courageously. In it, she invites the reader to allow the profound truth of scripture to travel from the head deep into the heart. I hope many, many people join Rhonda on this journey to explore the joys, sorrows, questions, and scriptures and learn to fall more in love with Jesus every day.

Jeff Myers
Corporate Trainer and Strength Coach

Rhonda has a deep love for God that has been rooted in family tradition and revitalized through her personal journey of brokenness and restoration—a healing that's still in the transformation process. Her desire for authentic connection invites you, the reader, on a journey of healing and wholeness yourself. Through honest reflection on your personal story, you will be given permission to submit to this process of curiosity and self-kindness that leads to renewed intimacy with God. If your expectations have ever been shattered and you find yourself searching for a solid foundation, pick up this book.

Mallory Albrecht
Life Group Director

When I heard the reality of Rhonda's story, I thought to myself that there is no way that this is real; she has too much joy! There are some people who use a trauma like this to trap themselves in a cycle of continued pain and bitterness; not Rhonda. She exudes the joy of the Lord—a true sign that healing has taken place. I pray that as you read this testimony it will help you find that same joy.

Tyler Hagan
Senior Pastor
Anthem Church Oakland

Contents

Acknowledgments

This book is dedicated to my family. Jason, you are my best friend and my rock; you have always supported my crazy dreams and allowed me to fulfill what God has called me to. Nina, I am so proud of the woman you are; thank you for being patient with me as I learned to be a mom and for being my social media guru. I would be lost without your ideas and support. Kalia, my beautiful girl who has brought laughter and joy into our lives, you will always be our rainbow baby because you came after quite the storm in our lives. Your joy, love, and passion for life inspires me to be the best version of myself! Tiana, my angel who inspires me, your brief life will always be remembered! We love you and will forever miss you!

To my parents, John and Lorraine Martinez, who have been a never-ending support and my prayer warriors through everything. To my co-host of *24 Carat Conversations* and my best friend, Phylis Mantelli: how would I do life without you? You have always been such a support, an ear when I needed you, and a shoulder to cry on!

Most of all, to Jesus, my Lord and Savior: this journey has not been easy, but You have held me tight through it all, and I am not sure how I could live life without You!

Foreword

There are people you meet in your lifetime that you instantly feel a spark with. There is that energy that draws you in and mesmerizes you. I felt that the day Rhonda joined our worship team at church. She was new to our small town, but a powerful presence as soon as she took the stage. I will admit, I was a bit jealous of that soulful voice when she practiced with us that afternoon. Something about her made me approach her after practice. I needed to know her better.

What started off as a casual conversation, soon grew to a deep open-hearted talk of our similar life stories. We found out we had both lost our babies after giving birth; she within hours and mine within 2 weeks. There is a "club" that you become a part of when losing a baby, and we were instantly bonded by our tragedies.

From that first day, I knew we would be close friends. What I did not expect was the life-long sisterhood that has become our life together. We joke that our friendship is like a marriage; we have had our ups and downs, but each time become closer when we work through the junk.

Rhonda and I grew up very differently. The things she expected out of her Christian home was so different than my difficult un-Christian home life. She taught me sound advice as I maneuvered through my Christian walk. Her advice was inspirational. Even though she is younger than me, her knowledge was invaluable. There was however in the beginning of our friendship a strict code that she often had. It was this sense that things should be blessed for her because she had been so faithful. I watched as she struggled with this in her other friendships, career, and motherhood.

What I have seen over the last fifteen years is a growth of maturity, compassion and love bursting out through the pain of life. Rhonda has become the gentle strength of a woman who understands God loves us all equally. God took her on a journey. A journey of which she leaned in and listened to His directive. What was once hardheartedness, turned into softness. Her listening ears became bigger, which in turn brought more people to her. I see her love for others in a way I never had before. She has always been sweet, but now there was understanding of other people's plight. She knows that we all are on the same path of finding our true passion and purpose. We may come from different backgrounds, some may have more than others or less, but the message is the same; God is here for all of us and wants us to draw closer to Him.

When she started on this writing journey, I was a bit surprised. She had never expressed an interest in doing so. I was so proud of her stepping out of her comfort zone to experience the things I had already journeyed through.

We decided in 2019 to start a Podcast together. We wanted to have a safe place to talk about issues most Christian women wanted to talk about. We wanted to support them and challenge them to discuss the hard topics. Our Podcast "24 Carat Conversation with Phylis and Rhonda" was born. It was instantly a hit among our friends and family in town. We laughed at what we were doing and how women loved it! We kept putting out episodes and within months the podcast grew and grew. We now have over 19,500 listeners (and growing) from all over the world. What started out as something to encourage women has become a movement of support and love. We took it one step further. When the Pandemic hit in 2020, we saw churches closing and clergy become paralyzed in fear. We did not know what the church would look like from here on out. Rhonda stepped into her God-given faith and said we needed to start an on-line Bible Study. I was not so sure. I followed her lead and we prayed for women to show up. They showed up, invited their friends, sisters, cousins, etc.

and then more. We continue to do the study to this day because God shows up and women are cared for.

I give acknowledgement to my best friend for that. Rhonda has a fierce spirit that does not give up. She has walked me through teary days and broken moments. She gives me strength when I feel hopeless. She will do the same for you.

Throughout this book you will be shaking your head in agreement over the rough times. You will cry along side her and cheer her on because it will give you the hope and strength to continue your journey.

I pray that this book helps you in your life journey to see that each day is a new day. To ponder where God has brought you before, and where He will take you in the future. Rhonda will be your guide to encourage you. I know she does for me.

Phylis Mantelli
Author, *Unmothered: Life with a Mom Who Couldn't Love Me*
Speaker, Coach, and Co-Host of the Podcast
24 Carat Conversations with Phylis and Rhonda

Introduction

This devotional is a compilation of twenty-four stories and encouragements for daily living. *24 Carat Conversations* is about real situations and real miracles that God has done in my life, and through this I hope that His refining process will bring forth gold in your life. I know that as Christians we have expectations of what our life should look like, and when our plans are foiled, we get discouraged; but I want you to be encouraged that no matter your situation, God is for you, and I pray that through these devotions you will find nuggets of gold and gems that you can hold on to! I will ask you each day to journal on a question that I prompt; this is so important, because you are going to begin to see how God works in your life.

Before we begin our journey, I want to take you back to where it all began.

John was a born into a dysfunctional family. His mom, a pastor's daughter, had rebelled and married a man who we found out had another family in another town. John's father was absent for most of his life. His mother, unable to care for John and his two sisters, gave them to his grandparents to raise. Having been abandoned by his mom, he dealt with lots of abandonment issues; his grandfather was a preacher and was very strict, like "couldn't-go-to-the-movies, wasn't-allowed-to-watch-TV" strict.

As a teen, he rebelled. One night he decided to go to a party, and he ended up spending the night at a friend's house after a night filled with drinking. In the morning, hungover, he arose to realize that it was Sunday, and if he wasn't in church his grandfather would be livid. His friend offered to drive him to the church—and being teenage boys, they decided to see how fast the 1952 Chevy would go. In a rural part of Colorado, the car hit gravel, and John flew out of the windshield of the car and into an irrigation ditch ten feet deep. He broke almost every bone in his body, tore the right side of his face to shreds, and was bleeding internally. The doctors gave him very little chance to live. His grandfather prayed over him, asking God to take him and not his grandson, as he hadn't lived a full life yet. John was unable to speak but heard everything his grandfather prayed over him. It was in that little hospital bed in Sterling, Colorado, that he decided to turn his whole life over to Jesus. He prayed, "God, if you heal me, I will serve you and I will dedicate my life to ministry." In a matter of days, John's condition had improved so much that the doctors could only explain it as a miracle. Within a week, John left the hospital with only broken bones and stitches in his face. God had healed him, and he dedicated his life to Jesus and broke the generational chains that had bound him. This is where his ministry journey began. He moved to California shortly after, where he met Lorraine Cortez.

Lorraine was born only seven miles from John in a small town in Colorado. Her grandmother had come to the Lord when she was instantly healed from rheumatoid arthritis. Her parents moved to California when she was just three years old. She was raised in a Christian home and accepted Jesus at the age of nine.

She met John shortly after he moved there from Colorado in the late 60s. He met her at a church service, and a short nine months later they married in April of 1970. I was born in July of 1973.

Why 24 Carat?

When I was trying to craft a name for both my devotional and the podcast, I wanted something that showed transparency and authenticity. I knew that twenty-four was the most precious and pure gold, and I also knew the process that any precious metal or stone endures when being refined. It is my hope that you will see the honesty and transparency in these devotionals. I also pray that it will help you refine who you are and help you look inward to see how to be the best version of you.

I have been told many times that carat's correct spelling is with a K (karat). And you're right; I chose the spelling carat because it encompasses both precious metals and stones. Carat, by definition, is actually the unit weight for precious stones and pearls, and the process of a pearl is like our lives: when a pearl is being formed, a grain of sand or a parasite enters into that oyster, and as a defense mechanism a fluid is released and coats it as a protectant, and then layer upon layer a pearl is formed.

In our lives we can have opposition, which is like the parasite or grain of sand: it can be irritating and abrasive. It is through that opposition that we become refined, like that fluid that washes over the pearl to reveal its beauty. Our lives will endure opposition, but as we are washed over and over, our beauty is then revealed.

Friends, if you are in opposition, and if life is feeling a little abrasive, remember that only the most beautiful things are made from that!

I hope this devotional inspires and encourages you.

Trouble

"For when he has tested me, I will come forth as gold"

(Job 23:10 NIV)

This scripture I have rooted deep in my heart. Sometimes we just can't understand why we are tested to such a severe degree and others seem to skate through life unscathed—or at least, it seems that way.

I have no other way than to take you back to my childhood. I am a second-generation pastor's daughter who grew up in church—Sunday morning, Sunday night, Wednesday night. I was part of the youth group and the choir, and involved in every church activity. When we weren't at church, we were traveling all over the state of California. My dad was the director of Teen Challenge and preached as I sang, week after week. These were the days when we didn't have iPhones or iPads. I spent a lot of time in the back seat of the car, listening to Elvis tunes and old worship music.

I am not complaining in any way—in fact, a lot of those memories are wonderful. I guess I figured with all the time I put in "serving God" that my life should be easy. I mean, I was a good girl who didn't get into too much trouble. Well, except for that one time I blew the engine of my car up while driving to Mexico with some boys from high school—oh, but that's a whole story in itself. I can honestly say that was the most rebellious thing I ever did, and I got into so much trouble I never wanted to experience that again.

The trials I have experienced over the last decade or two have definitely hit me hard. I think my expectation of who God was and how He was supposed to favor me over others was not realistic. Who did I think I was? I mean, Job was blameless and upright and suffered, so I am not sure why I thought life was going to hand me special treatment.

I have learned that whether you grew up in the church or not, good person or bad, life hits and sometimes it hits hard. We try to rationalize the whys and what ifs. We can't wrap our brain around why someone died unexpectedly, why we ended up alone after we married someone we thought was our soulmate, why our business failed, or why our child died. The list can go on and on.

We may feel abandoned by God, like He has left us to suffer, but I can tell you that He is right there. We may not see it or feel it, but when we can't stand, He is holding us up. We need to learn that as long as we are here on this earth, we will have trouble. In John 16:33 (NIV) it says, "I have told you these things, so that in me you may have peace. In this world you will have trouble. But take heart! I have overcome the world." Let's examine that. *You will* have trouble. He is not guaranteeing a perfect life; in fact, if we are being honest, the more you start to work toward being a better you, you can bet that the enemy is going to attack. Why? Because he knows your potential and he wants you to stay angry, bitter, and upset. If the enemy can put a wedge between you and God, then he knows he can start to fill your mind with those things that aren't true. Our mind is a battlefield, and we have to know how to fight our battles—in prayer, in fasting, in spending time with God. Even if we are feeling resentment toward our situation, we must press through and declare that He is good, even in midst of our circumstances.

So, let's remember this: God is on our side. He wants to see us flourish, but we live in an imperfect world, so we will have trouble. But He has overcome the world and we need to stand firm on His promises.

RESPOND Day 1:

Journal about a struggle you have had recently. Think about how that has made you feel. Abandoned by God? Upset with God? Be honest and open in your thoughts.

Now think about a past struggle and how God brought you through that; write it down and reflect on the goodness of God.

The Wait

"Wait for the Lord; be strong and let your heart take courage; yes, wait for the Lord"

(Psalm 27:14 NASB)

I guess you could say that I lived a bit of a sheltered life. I thought that life, especially Christian life, had a certain path, so humor me. If you grew up in church you will know this thought process, and if not—well, I am going to explain.

You grow up in church, go off to Bible college, meet the man of your dreams. You get married, have kids, and you might even be in ministry—a pastor, a youth pastor, or a church leader in some capacity. If you grew up as a pastor's kid, you may even think that you are going to be called to ministry because that's the way it is supposed to work, and—*duh*—your parents are pastors. Let's just say I had lot of expectations of how things were supposed to be, and that was not necessarily reality.

Well, mine didn't quite work that way. I did go off to Bible college and got my degree in addiction studies, but I didn't meet the man of my dreams (at least, not yet). I did meet a man who happened to be in Teen Challenge—oh, he was a beautiful man of Portuguese descent, with green eyes and curly hair, and I thought, *Oh, this must be the man God wants me to be with!* So, I decided that dating him was justified—I wanted what I wanted and the vision that I had in my head. I didn't listen to God's warnings or God's prompts. Yes, this man at the time was following Jesus, but he was also a drug addict, and with that came a lot of other issues that couldn't just be ignored. Let's just say that my parents were 100 percent against this relationship, but my mom was adamant in supporting me—she told me later that it was because she didn't want me going off and rebelling because they were not in favor of it.

We got engaged on Christmas of 1993. We were planning the wedding for the fall of 1994. As the date approached, he finished rehab and began to go back to his life—a life I thought we would live together. He had a five-year-old daughter and she lived in another town, so he moved back there to be with her. Between December and May something changed in him, and I could see it, but I just didn't want to believe it. On the day of my graduation from college, he was supposed to meet me at the church where the ceremony was being held, but he didn't show up. I remember sitting in my seat, stretching my neck to see if he was there, and then walking across that stage, squinting to see if he had shown—but there was no sign of him. After the ceremony, he did show up and said he was there, but I later found out that he had lied and wasn't there until the end of the ceremony. It was an awkward car ride back to my parents' where they were planning a celebration, but before we went, he wanted to talk to me. We stopped at a park near my house, and there I was with my cap and gown in my hands. He broke the news that he had cheated on me with his ex-girlfriend, the mother of his child, and that he was using drugs again, and he called off the engagement. I was devastated and broken. I remember going home and literally falling on my face in the hallway, crying uncontrollably.

How could God let this happen to me? I was so upset with God, and not to mention embarrassed that I was going to have to share with everyone that the wedding was off.

Now I tell you this story because I wanted what I wanted. I didn't care that God had said not to marry him, and I still accepted the proposal. I had seen signs but chose to ignore them, because I wanted this fantasy life that I thought was supposed to be. Sometimes our timing isn't God's timing; sometimes He has something so much better, but we are willing to settle for less-than because we think we aren't worthy of what He has for us. In my situation, I believe that God protected me from a very hard life that I would have led with an addict. He had better for me, but I just couldn't see it.

Maybe for you it isn't a broken engagement—maybe it's a job you want, or a relationship that you desire to have to fill a void. Whatever it is, I encourage you to wait for what He has for you. It's hard, and the wait isn't always easy, but if we want God's best, we need to be secure in knowing that He has the best for us, and that in the waiting He can grow us into who He wants us to be.

RESPOND Day 2:

Have you ever had a situation where you knew that God had better, but you ignored His voice?

How did it end up?

What did you learn?

What did God protect you from?

Hope and Future

"'For I know the plans and thoughts that I have for you,' says the Lord, 'plans for peace and well-being and not for disaster, to give you a future and a hope'"
(Jeremiah 29:11 AMP)

It's amazing how nine months can change your life. Since my broken engagement I had reevaluated myself and moved into a tiny apartment down the street from my home that I grew up in. I felt like I needed to figure things out and grow up a bit. I'm not sure that was the best idea, as I ended up living paycheck to paycheck and rarely ate because I had no money, but nonetheless I grew up really quickly.

I was working two jobs so I could pay off college debt and still be on my own: working part time for my dad at Teen Challenge as a counselor and part time at a local grocery store. On my second day there I ran into a familiar face from high school. I wasn't very popular in high school—my dad was a minister, so that didn't get you into the cool crowd—but I did remember this guy. He was on the same wrestling team as my high school ex-boyfriend, and I remembered thinking he was kind of cute but had never bothered to really ever speak to him.

As we began to work together and talk from time to time on breaks, I grew in fondness for him. He was nice, and I thought maybe I'd go on a date with him, so when he asked, I said yes. We went on one date and I decided *Nope, not my type, and I never want to see him again,* except for at work of course. This guy wouldn't give up. One day he called me and asked if I wanted to see a movie at my place—well, that was a big no, so I told him no; but he had roommates, so I felt comfortable to say, "I can go over your place to watch a movie." He then said, "Well, I don't have a VCR." Yeah, it was a long time ago, and way before DVDs or downloaded movies. I was quite feisty and said, "Well, go buy one then," and hung the phone up.

Not kidding—thirty minutes later he called back to tell me he had bought a VCR, and was I coming to watch a movie now? Well, what could I say? I said yes, and the rest is history; we will be married twenty-five years this year.

Sometimes we go through difficulties and struggles, and we can't see God's best for us. Had I married that other man, who knows how life would have turned out?

God had Jason waiting for me, but I had to trust God's plan, not mine. When our plans don't work out, we often think God has abandoned us or He doesn't care about us, but that's just not true. Oftentimes He is protecting us from something, because as the verse says, He wants to give us a hope and a future.

When you feel like you are in the eye of life's storms, know that the overwhelming, all-consuming situation is in His hands. He wants the best for you and your future; trust that process, and trust that He knows best. Now I am not saying that life is a cakewalk, because as you will see, just because God gave me an amazing husband doesn't mean that our life hasn't been quite a rollercoaster. And I can tell you that if God had shown me everything we would endure, I might have been like the runaway bride, because the storms we have endured over the last twenty-five years have not been easy—but His plans are so much better than mine!

RESPOND Day 3:

Have you been struggling with a plan that doesn't seem to be working out in your favor? Or maybe you feel called to something He has for you but are scared that it might not work out—are you trusting His plan? If not, why not? What are your fears?

Comparison Kills

"I know what it is to be in need, and I know what it is to have plenty. I have learned the secret of being content in any and every situation, whether well fed or hungry, whether living in plenty or in want. I can do all this through him who gives me strength"
(Philippians 4:12-13 NIV)

Sometimes the dream seems way better than the reality. We had a beautiful wedding and honeymooned in Cabo San Lucas, Mexico. Upon our return, not only did I have the worst bout of sickness, but two days after we got home my husband got laid off from his job and my car got broken into. I look back now and it's almost comical, but for a newly married couple this was stressful and would be the first of many journeys down the road of life.

We managed to get through all of it, and my husband shortly after found another job—one he liked much better. I then found out that I was pregnant; we had both always wanted children, so we were excited to be journeying this road.

Our daughter Nina was born in January, and we began the journey of parenthood. Although I can say that during that time it was wonderful and we settled into parenthood, we also had our fair share of fumbling through married life, parenthood, and working full time. I had a lot of friends who were also new parents, but most of my girlfriends were able to stay home full time, something that I thought at the time I really wanted. I often say that I am a recovering coveter—you know, I was jealous of what everyone else had. I wanted the house with a yard, a nice SUV, and to be home full time with my daughter. That just wasn't our life, and I had to work. I enjoyed working but felt like a bit of a failure as a mom because I couldn't be home full time.

God really convicted me one day as I was reeling with jealousy over a couple who were friends of ours and who had just bought a new home. I heard God so clearly say, "Be content in what you have right now; I can't bless you with more when you are so jealous of others." That was such a huge revelation, and I knew right then and there that I needed to be grateful for this life that God had given me, and that He knew everything I needed.

Jealousy keeps us from God's best; I learned that firsthand. It may seem as though someone has more, or that they are living better—and especially in this world today, where social media just shows the best of everyone. How many times have you scrolled through someone's Instagram feed and seen them snapping a picture of their new car or home, or that fabulous vacation you wish you could be on? We need to remember, that is not our season or even our story. Sometimes it is hard to be happy for someone who seems to have everything, while you sit and work and don't have that same lifestyle.

I know that during that season I learned that God is my provider, and I need to be grateful for what He has given me. When I do, I open myself up to the greater things that He has for me—it may not always be monetary things, and it may just be the simplest things in life. But today, I challenge you to look at what you have and be grateful for the season and place you are in right now. If you can be grateful now, when you are blessed you will appreciate and enjoy that gift so much more.

RESPOND Day 4:

Write down three things that you are grateful for and why you are grateful for them.

Spend some time reflecting on the blessings God has given you right now, in this season, and ask God to help you not to compare yourself with others.

The Church and Betrayal

"Lord, hear my prayer, listen to my cry for mercy; in your faithfulness and righteousness come to my relief"

(Psalm 143:1 NIV)

After Jason and I married, my parents went through a very difficult time with the church. I watched my parents being treated poorly by church leadership. I remember feeling a sense of betrayal, and I just couldn't understand how the church could hurt their own. My father was so burned out from ministry, and he made some very bad decisions, but instead of lifting him up they chose to betray him. We were all affected by this.

I was newly married, and yes, it took a toll on my marriage. My brother was unable to go to a university he wanted to go to because of all of the scandal, my mother was on the verge of a nervous breakdown, and things were very grim. I remember thinking, *Where are you, God? Why are you allowing such pain?*

I believe that we were in a place of warfare, and we all felt defeated. Satan used that scandal to bury us, but my mom in her weak state still got on her knees every day prayed and asked God to restore what had been lost. I guess you could say that I felt as though we were living the book of Job. In life we often feel that the pain and the hurt will never be healed, or that we will never walk in restoration. I want you to know that no matter what you have been through, what you have done, there is nothing you can do that can make Jesus turn His back on you. You may be in a dark place today; you may feel alone and as though you can never be restored, but Jesus is the King of restoration. I can tell you now, looking back twenty-five years later, that we have still endured some pretty difficult times, but God has brought us through this, and what Satan deemed for bad God used for good.

Recently I was visiting my brother on vacation, and we had a discussion about how hurt we had been by this incident. Now this was over twenty-five years ago, but although the wounds had healed, you could still feel them like a scar. We shed tears as we stood in his kitchen, remembering those very dark moments. As my brother and I talked through the pain of that situation in our lives, we also came to realize that, had certain events not happened, we wouldn't be where we are today! Had he gone to that university he so desired, he would have never met his wife. God's faithfulness carried us through it, and today we can stand, saying that even though that time was dark, we can trust Him to be faithful to restore and heal.

RESPOND Day 5:

Have you ever felt betrayed by people who you felt were supposed to support you?

Have you ever felt isolated or hurt by the church or people in the church community?

List out what hurt you, name it, and then write "I release this to you, Jesus."

What can you do to not get bitter but get better if you have been hurt? Forgiveness starts with you!

The Unexpected

He said I wouldn't be crushed:

"We are hard pressed on every side, but not crushed; perplexed, but not in despair; persecuted, but not abandoned; struck down, but not destroyed"
(2 Corinthians 4:8-9 NIV)

As you now know, I had this idea in my head of what my life should have looked like—and honestly, up to this point life had let me down, but never like the next season I would endure.

We had just moved into a cute little blue house in the Bay Area and felt like we were just getting back on our feet. I was working for a new company and really felt like we had hit our stride. I had just found out that I was pregnant, and we were very excited for a new addition to our family. My oldest was four, and this age difference was just perfect.

As the fall approached, my belly began to grow, and the anticipation of another child was so exciting. On September 11, 2001, America had the largest terrorist attack in history. I remember thinking, *Oh my gosh, what am I doing bringing a child into this world?* I was just sickened by this, and fear began to rise in me. At the same time, I began to not feel very well but was encouraged by the doctors that each pregnancy was very different and that all looked good. I had this gut feeling that something was wrong but couldn't get anyone to listen to me.

We entered the New Year with lots of expectations; we were planning baby showers, shopping for baby items, and getting our eldest, Nina, ready to be a big sister. As the months progressed, the feeling that something was wrong got stronger, and I got sicker. I couldn't pinpoint what it was, but everything in me hurt. I was helping my boss get his business up and running, so I just kept chalking it up to the fact that I was working too hard. I remember so clearly going to a wedding on Valentine's Day and not even being able to sit for an hour, my back was in so much pain. Again, the doctors couldn't pinpoint anything, so it was just dismissed.

On March 18, 2002, I remember just feeling sick, but I had so much work on my desk, I had to go in. My husband was upset with me that morning because he wanted me to stay home, but this stubborn Latina wasn't having it, so I pushed through. I got to the office early that morning; no one was there yet. The pains began and started to get stronger. By this time a coworker came in and I told her, "I think I'm in labor." She immediately called my husband and told him to meet us at the hospital. As she drove up to the entrance of the hospital, there was my husband with the video camera in hand, ready to video the birth of our newest addition to our family.

We entered the hospital and got checked in, and they strapped the monitor onto my belly. I could hear the heartbeat and was just so excited to welcome our new baby. The look on the doctor's face told me differently; she kept moving the monitor around and losing the heartbeat. I asked, "Is everything okay?" Her response was, "We keep losing her heartbeat; I am going to get a specialist in here to look." My heart dropped, and I knew something was wrong. My husband called my parents, who rushed over to the hospital right away. I clearly remember having a conversation with my mom, telling her, "If this baby dies, I don't want to live." The thought of not bringing my daughter home was something I thought I just couldn't do. Hours progressed, and they still couldn't get a clear heartbeat and had finally decided on a C-section. Now this was something I didn't want, but at that point I just wanted to see my baby, so I agreed. The next events are a bit blurry, and I am not sure if that is because of the medication or just because my heart and mind can't take in all the pain I endured that day. A few very short hours after I gave birth, my daughter Tiana died of a heart condition in my husband's arms.

Crushed, bruised, perplexed, just like that verse in 2 Corinthians. My dreams were crushed, bruised, and I was perplexed; how could this happen to us? I mean, I was a good Christian girl, I had done everything right—what was God doing? I have learned that often I don't understand His purpose, but I do know that there is a purpose to the pain we endure. We just need to lean into trusting Him completely.

RESPOND Day 6:

Have you ever experienced loss (job loss, loss of a child, loss of a parent, divorce)?

How did it make you feel?

Did you blame God? Can you find a purpose in your painful experience?

Empty-Handed and Crushed

"The Lord is close to the brokenhearted and saves those who are crushed in spirit"

(Psalm 34:18 NIV)

I remember the pain in my heart that I felt, leaving the hospital empty-handed, broken, and wondering when this pain would stop. This all felt like a dream, like it never happened; but I felt the pain in my belly where I had the C-section, and my arms ached to hold my baby. We had not a second to grieve just yet; we were in the middle of planning a funeral—not exactly how I pictured this to be. Again, I felt so let down by God.

What had I done to deserve this? We were just getting back on our feet, and now this? I felt so discouraged and depressed, but I couldn't stop. I had a four-year-old daughter who needed me to be there for her and a husband who was grieving too, although his grief was not showing the way mine was. This was causing a wedge between us, and I felt so alone.

The first week of grief is interesting—you have people reaching out, bringing you meals, asking if you need help, but as the weeks progress you are still in grief, and everyone else has moved on. You are stuck in this cycle of pain, and it even feels strange to laugh when something is funny. It's like being in a daze and not being able to snap out of it.

I remember so clearly this one morning, about four days after the funeral. I was snuggled up in bed with Nina and we were just going to stay right there all day, watching cartoons—whatever she wanted. I knew she was grieving too, and I wanted her right by my side. As I clicked on the TV, it wasn't working; I tried to turn the lights on—nothing. I thought, *Oh, no, did I forget to pay the electric bill? In all the chaos, maybe I forgot.* I rummaged through a pile of mail, and there it was: a notice from the City saying that on that day, March 27, the power would be out from 8:00-2:00 for construction. The only thing worse than grief is grief in complete silence. I remember just crying and trying to not let Nina see that I was sad. I played with her the best I could, as I was still healing from the C-section, and the pain of losing my daughter was so raw.

In the quietness of that morning, as I opened my Bible and began to journal, that's when healing began. I knew that I could trust Jesus. I knew that He knew what was best for me, and I knew that I had to lean on Him for complete emotional healing.

If you are in a season that is difficult, you need to find the time to be quiet with your thoughts. It's a loud world out there, friends, and we must find the time to be quiet with God and allow Him to begin to work in us.

RESPOND Day 7:

If you're struggling right now, how can you find time to get quiet with God?

Take five minutes right now to tell God what you are struggling with.

Take five to ten minutes today to spend time with God; talk to Him like you would to your best friend. Stay quiet in His presence so you can hear His voice.

The Aftermath

"For he will command his angels concerning you to guard you in all your ways. On their hands they will bear you up, lest you strike your foot against a stone"

(Psalm 91:11-12 ESV)

I love this verse; I am a very visual person, so humor me. In this verse I can imagine a glorious, beautiful angel with huge wings covering me and guarding me as I take steps in life, and when I almost misstep, that angel is there to hold me up and protect me. The verse says in *all my ways*—that means the good and the bad.

In the days and months following my daughter Tiana's death we endured some pretty tough emotional stumbling blocks. My husband was not grieving like me, and honestly, I felt really alone. He was working lots of hours and had really shut me out emotionally. I then had three of my best girlfriends pregnant at the same time as me. Just two short weeks after I had Tiana, one of my best girlfriends at the time gave birth to her daughter—talk about crushing. I felt devastated. Now I was happy for her, but I was also bitter and upset that my daughter wasn't here. I wanted to fast-forward my life and move to a better part; this was miserable, and I felt like time was standing still and everyone was moving fast around me.

I had eight weeks of maternity leave from my job, and honestly, I was anxious to get back to work. Eight weeks hardly seems like enough time to grieve the loss of a child, but that was about all the time we could afford to let me take off. I felt like if I went back to work, things would magically fall into place, and I would feel better about the journey life had taken me on.

Shortly after returning to work, I walked in one early morning to find my severance package letter on the photo copy machine. All I could think was, *You have got to be kidding me!* I walked straight into my boss's office and asked him, "What is this?" Not even looking me in the face, his response was cold as he said, "I think you just need more time to grieve." I was devastated and beside myself. I packed my desk up into cardboard boxes, got in my car, and cried all the way home.

Grief is a journey—a journey that takes you down a road of ups and downs and where every day is different. One day I would feel completely fine, and the next I was feeling like a total mess. During this time, I realized that this journey was going to be much more challenging than I expected. This is when I realized that if I didn't face this head on, I was going to slip into a depression. I knew that God had a plan and purpose for all of this pain, but I just couldn't see it—and honestly, I was really mad at God. As I explained earlier, I feel like my expectations of God and Christianity were not realistic. I think that growing up in church, I just expected that things were going to be smooth sailing, and my life had been nothing like that up to this point. So I continued to struggle in my faith and understanding of why a good God would let me endure such pain. It is the hope of the plans He has laid out for my life that has kept me going when the grief swallows me under.

RESPOND Day 8:

Have you ever struggled with depression? If so, were you embarrassed to address or admit it?

Have you experienced grief? What are some of the ways you dealt with it?

What can you learn from your grief?

How can you rely on God when struggling with hard situations?

Grief and Finding Comfort

"God blesses those people who grieve. They will find comfort!"

(Matthew 5:4 CEV)

For anyone who has experienced the deep pain of grief, you can relate that the days seem long, and the nights seem longer. I spent many nights crying and praying, wondering where God was in all of this—2002 seemed like the longest year of my life. We had been to genetic doctors who confirmed that we could in fact have another baby with about a 90 percent chance of no issues. We were incredibly excited to have been given the green light to try again.

Trying again wasn't all that easy; month after month, I was disappointed. I had never had any problem getting pregnant, but it wasn't happening. I was beginning to feel a little discouraged. On March 18, 2003—exactly one year from the date Tiana had passed—I took a pregnancy test, and it was positive. We were so excited to be expecting again. The months that passed were tough; if you have ever been through loss of pregnancy, you know that it is scary to try again. I was due in December, but my doctor agreed to induce me in November, because I was paranoid to go past thirty-seven weeks. The day I was scheduled to deliver, I remember so clearly our pastors from our church coming to pray over us. I would be lying if I said that I wasn't fearful that day; I couldn't imagine losing another child. At that moment I remembered my months of trying to conceive, asking God to bless us with another baby. One night as I was praying and journaling, I remember hearing so clearly in my spirit: "Nina came to restore your family, and this baby is coming to complete you." You see, in 1998 when Nina was born, my parents were going through that incredibly trying time and were really struggling in their marriage. Nina brought hope and peace to that situation, and honestly, I believe she helped heal their marriage.

On November 16, 2003, Kalia Katherine Hope was born. We were very intentional with her name. **Kalia** in Hawaiian means beautiful; **Hope** because she brought so much hope into our lives. Katherine was the name of our doctor who delivered our daughter Tiana; she also helped me walk through the pregnancy with Kalia, so when she was born we felt we needed to incorporate

Dr. Katherine Brubaker's name in with Kalia's. She had been such a God-given blessing to us, and Dr. Brubaker had become a big part of our lives. I believe God allowed her to be there the day Tiana passed—she was a high-risk doctor and just happened to be doing rounds that day. God knew that we needed her to help us go through the pregnancy with Kalia, so for that reason, we decided we must honor her name.

In my grief, God sprinkled blessings that I would have never imagined. I know that at times we wonder where He is, why He is making us wait; it doesn't make sense. I want to encourage you today that He is there; He is with you even through your darkest times.

RESPOND Day 9:

How has God shown His mercy to you through times of grief and loss?

Can you name God's goodness in the midst of a tough season?

Trauma

*"The Lord is near to the brokenhearted and saves
the crushed in spirit. Many are the afflictions of the
righteous, but the Lord delivers him out of them all"*
(Psalm 34:18-19 ESV)

Kind of funny how something that happened in the
past can sneak up and bite you when you least expect
it. I never realized that the trauma of losing my daughter, and of other things I had endured in life, would
seep back in and leave some deep wounds. I honestly
thought I was okay.

It was a fall evening, and I could feel sadness filling
my heart. I had been struggling with this sadness for a
while; in fact, I had started detaching from friendships,
not wanting to go out or do things with anyone. I wish
I could pinpoint what started making me feel anxious
and sad, but quite honestly, I didn't know why it was
happening. I remember one night so clearly hearing
in my head, "No one cares about you," "God has aban-

doned you," "Your family would be better off without you." Clear as day I heard this voice. It was the voice of the enemy, telling me that I wasn't enough! I remember getting up off the couch and walking upstairs into my room. Normally the closet is where I go to get quiet and pray, but on this night, I walked into that closet with those voices in my head telling me that I wasn't enough, feeling exhausted and just done with life.

If you have ever experienced depression on that level, you will know that as much as you try to shake that voice from the enemy, it is hard. As I walked into that dark closet, I could see a purple scarf swinging from my clothing rod as if it was enticing me. I thought, *What if I just wrapped this scarf around my neck? Then it would all be over.* I dropped to my knees and began crying out to God. I was starting to feel my chest tighten, I felt breathless, and I began to shake uncontrollably, lying on the floor in fetal position. I was in a full-blown panic attack—so much so that I passed out. When I awoke, there I was on the floor, with my husband and a fireman asking if I was okay, checking my vitals.

The last thing I remembered was falling to my knees in utter desperation and asking God to help me stop these thoughts and to quiet my mind. Here I was, a pastor's kid who was actually thinking about taking her own life. Now that seems super selfish, and I knew those thoughts weren't of God, but what I learned was that I hadn't healed from the trauma of my daughter's death, the trauma of the betrayal of the church, and the aftermath of my parents' struggles after that betrayal that affected all of us. I was still living this expectation of having to be perfect. I was trying to make it all look good, and heaven forbid I ever admit to being sad or depressed. I had stuffed my emotions and feelings and just didn't deal with any of it, because I thought that was what good pastor's kids did—we just prayed and asked God to put a Band-Aid on it and hoped we could pray it away! That absolutely isn't how we heal from our trauma. God wants us to open up those wounds and seek counsel, and God wants to heal us from the inside out! He wants us to be transparent with Him; He already knows our struggles, but we must release them to Him if we want to be healed.

In the months and years after that night, I sought counseling and worked hard on understanding how to cope when I would get overwhelmed. I admitted that anxiety and depression was something that I struggled with, and it was okay. I learned how to manage it and how to deal with it when I started to spiral. I learned ways to cope, and in the process, learned that it's okay to talk about my struggle with no shame, no fear of judgment. The greatest thing about coming to this place was that I learned that my story would help others who struggled with the same thing.

RESPOND Day 10:

Are you holding on to something in your past that you feel shame about? Now write down what you are feeling shameful about, and next to it write what lie is associated with that shame.

Coming Out of the Dark

"The light shines in the darkness, and the darkness has not overcome it"

(John 1:5 NIV)

Darkness in the Bible means misery. God sent his Son Jesus so that He could save us from this; He is the light of the world. When we are in darkness, He is our light.

In the last few weeks, we have been in a "shelter in place" due to the COVID-19 virus, and it feels dark; it feels as though we will never see the light again.

As I was pondering that thought, I was reminded of a morning a few months back in Montecito, California. I got up early to walk the beach and as dawn began to break, I could hear birds begin to chirp. It was dark, then all of a sudden the sky began to lighten and hues of pink, yellow, and orange began to emerge. It was absolutely breathtaking!

Maybe today you are feeling as though you are in the darkest hour of your life, and you aren't convinced that you will see the light of day anytime soon. I want to encourage you that the darkness will break, and we will see light again.

Let me encourage you, friends, that often it is through the darkness of life that we are given chances to grow, and often that darkness brings perspective that we can't see in the light.

I know that embracing the dark times in our life is hard, but stay the course and know that you will see the light again. When it breaks through, you will look back and see how those dark times shaped you and how much you grew.

RESPOND Day 11:

Are you able to see God's light in the midst of darkness?

If not, why, and what is holding you back from seeing His goodness?

How can you work toward having a positive outlook even in the midst of the storm?

Rest

"And he said, 'My presence will go with you, and I will give you rest'"

(Exodus 33:14 ESV)

The last eighteen years have been quite a whirl-wind—between growing my career, being involved in church ministry life, raising kids, and starting a podcast, it has been really busy. I remember at the beginning of the year praying, "God, I just need rest." On March 17, 2020, we were informed of a "shelter in place" order due to the COVID-19 virus—not exactly the rest I was looking for—so if I am to blame for that prayer, I am sorry for asking for rest! I find that my mind often needs a reset. I can tend to get into the busyness of life, and it can cause me to become overwhelmed. Now I was hoping for more like a tropical vacation than a pandemic, but this season has really put my faith to the test.

You see, things don't always go as planned and often we pray and fast, hoping for a quick answer—and it's crickets. We begin to question where God is and what He is doing. During this time, I was praying specifically for something that was very heavy on my heart. I prayed, fasted, and felt completely exhausted after forty days of earnest prayer. I called a friend one night just bawling, and quite frankly at wits' end, and she said, "Rhonda, you have done your part; I think it's okay to rest now, rest and know that God sees your heart and hears your prayers, and He's working." As I write this today, my prayer is yet to be answered, but I will tell you this: in the midst of whatever God is doing, He is asking that I rest in His arms and let Him figure out the details.

RESPOND Day 12:

Is it hard for you to rest and trust that God is working?

How does it make you feel when you are hearing nothing from God?

Write down what you are waiting on God for; now verbally release it to Him and rest.

Trust Issues

Shortly before dawn Jesus went out to them, walking on the lake. When the disciples saw him walking on the lake, they were terrified. "It's a ghost," they said, and cried out in fear.

But Jesus immediately said to them: "Take courage! It is I. Don't be afraid."

"Lord, if it's you," Peter replied, "tell me to come to you on the water."

"Come," he said.

Then Peter got down out of the boat, walked on the water and came toward Jesus. But when he saw the wind, he was afraid and, beginning to sink, cried out, "Lord, save me!" Immediately Jesus reached out his hand and caught him. "You of little faith," he said, "why did you doubt?"

Matthew 14:25-31 (NIV)

Am I the only one with trust issues? I hope not!

A few months back I went to an intensive self-development and leadership course for three days. I had been really digging into my past hurts and pain and wanted to do some deep healing in my heart. One morning, on the second day of the course, the leader read the passage about Peter walking on water. She asked us to imagine where we were in that story, and quite honestly, I couldn't even get out of the boat. As I sat there, anxiety began to fill my heart—why couldn't I trust Jesus and get out of the boat?

The leader then asked, "Where are you in that story?" I raised my hand and said, "I can't get out of the boat." She then asked, "Why?" As I began to speak, tears streamed down my face. You see, I thought I had trusted Jesus with everything, but the fact is, I hadn't; I had let the past hurt and pain cloud my vision on seeing His faithfulness. I took my eyes off of Him, scared He wouldn't be there to hold my hand through it. Here I was, a kid who grew up in church, who knew every Bible story, but I didn't trust Jesus. I thought I did, but I was realizing that healing in my own heart had to begin and those broken places needed to truly heal.

That day was what I would call a transformation moment. Trusting God isn't always easy; it's a daily practice that I must press into, and I won't lie—often I get frustrated by the waves of life. I am working every day to trust Him in the midst of the storm, but I also validate the feelings of being scared if it doesn't work out the way I see it should. What I do know is that each time I take one step closer to my Lord and Savior, He is there, arms stretched out, waiting for me to look into His eyes. To trust that He is good, and that He is faithful to carry us through our deepest pain and trials.

RESPOND Day 13:

What pain are you enduring right now?

Are you able to envision yourself walking to Him and trusting Him with your pain?

In the Pressing

"Neither is new wine put into old wineskins. If it is, the skins burst and the wine is spilled and the skins are destroyed. But new wine is put into fresh wineskins, and so both are preserved"

(Matthew 9:17 ESV)

We visited this beautiful winery in Napa Valley. The sommelier explained each wine, and the process of the crushing and pressing of the wine, and the time it spends in the barrels. Some of the wines are preserved in dark caves to continue the fermentation process and won't be released until a later date. We were able to sample a cave wine, and the difference was noticeable from the younger-aged wine. The complex flavor of the aged wine was smooth like silk to our palates, and while the younger wine was delicious, you could taste how the aging process of the older wine made it burst with flavor.

I was reminded of that song called "New Wine." It talks about being pressed and crushed and being made into new wine through that process of trials and tribulations.

This year has felt crushing, as we have been pressed on every side. Maybe you feel like that wine that's in a dark cave, waiting to be opened, wondering where God is in this process. Know this: He is working on you, and in time you will emerge from that cave, changed and stronger than ever!

I know that it's through the crushing and pressing of life that we are made stronger. We must trust the process and know that God is in control of every situation. It's in the surrender into our heavenly Father's hands that we are able to see that He is purifying us, preparing us for greater things. We can't rush the process; we must be patient, trusting completely in Him.

RESPOND Day 14:

What does the pressing process in your life look like right now?

How did God bring you through a pressing in your past? Remembering His faithfulness in our hard, pressing seasons can remind us that He will come through again and again.

Trials and Temptations

"Consider it pure joy, my brothers and sisters, whenever you face trials of many kinds, because you know that the testing of your faith produces perseverance. Let perseverance finish its work so that you may be mature and complete, not lacking anything"
(James 1:2-4 NIV)

I have often said, "Endure to emerge." I am not sure about you, but to me enduring isn't easy—that word sounds like a ton of work, right? *Endure* sounds like barely surviving, and lots of pain and disappointment. Often, that is how it feels when we are facing trials in our lives. I am taken back to a few months ago when we had a trial in our family, and every morning I would wake thinking, *Ugh, it's morning, and I have to endure this today; I was hoping it was a bad dream.* My attitude was definitely not great about this situation, and I had to surrender every day my negative mindset in order to press through. As I pondered James 1:2-4, I realized that there was some place in my life that God was working on, and He needed me to persevere in order for Him to complete His work in me. As I talked about at the beginning, anything beautiful has most likely come through a process of enduring; we can't just expect life to be perfect and to never endure the hard stuff. If it was, we wouldn't ever grow in maturity as humans or as Christians.

I found myself during this season asking God, "What are you teaching me?" "What do I need to learn in this season?" Quite frankly, friends, it was the only way I was able to endure the season of sadness that had fallen on my family. I embraced the trial and asked God to each day give me the grace, patience, and ability to get through it. I am still nowhere near an expert at this, but I am trying every day to see what's emerging out of the endurance.

RESPOND Day 15:

What life circumstance are you enduring or have you endured?

Do you see how you emerged after enduring? What good can you see that came of it?

If you're still in the trial, can you take a few minutes to write it down and surrender it to Him? Then verbally say, "I surrender (whatever your situation is) to you, Jesus."

Broken and Beautiful

*"My sacrifice, O God, is a broken spirit; a broken
and contrite heart you, God, will not despise"*
(Psalm 51:17 NIV)

I remember a day not long ago, when we had been
going through a really difficult time and I was prayed
out and exhausted. I had received some distress-
ing news and ran upstairs to my bedroom closet and
slammed the door. For those of you who don't know, I
pray *a lot* in my closet—it's quiet and dark, and I feel like
I hear God's voice there the most. Well, this day in particular I ran in there, and as I slammed the door I heard
a crackling of glass. I looked back, only to see that I had
slammed the door so hard that the glass had cracked
both inside and outside of the closet door. I immediately felt such shame—I didn't mean to slam it so hard;
I was just so distraught that I slammed it with force. I

burst into tears and fell on the floor; I couldn't believe that I had just done that. As I sat quietly, reflecting on what had just happened, all I could hear was: "It's okay to be beautifully broken." You see, the news I had heard that day had shattered my heart the way that glass had shattered on the door. God uses the broken things in our lives and is able to make beauty from it. During the seasons of brokenness, Satan often uses shame and guilt to tell us that we aren't enough, we aren't beautiful, we aren't worthy. What if, in the brokenness, God is using it to create something beautiful?

If we had it all together, we wouldn't have any need for Jesus. It's in the brokenness of our situations that He sits with us on the floor—as we are crying, as mascara runs down our face—and holds us. He holds our tears and our pain and says that imperfect is okay, that the feelings we have are valid, and that it's okay not to have it "all together."

I am confident that our broken stories will reveal beauty, and although we are unable to see it while we are sitting in the pain, God has promised to sustain us through our struggles! So, friends, be encouraged that being beautifully broken is a place of full surrender; fall into His arms and know that it's His strength that will carry us through.

RESPOND Day 16:

What does "broken yet beautiful" look like for you?

Are you able to see God's faithfulness through the journey of struggle?

Take a few minutes to write your beautifully broken story.

Heart Transplant

"And I will give you a new heart, and a new spirit I
will put within you. And I will remove the heart of
stone from your flesh and give you a heart of flesh"
(Ezekiel 36:26 ESV)

There are many types of heart surgeries, but the most complex is a heart transplant. A heart transplant is the last resort to get the heart working again. It means removing and replacing a diseased heart with a healthy one. When you need a new heart, it requires a donor and a skilled and experienced surgeon to conduct the surgery without any negative impact on the person receiving the new heart.

I had a friend who was going through a major marriage issue, and she just couldn't seem to see what God was doing. Her husband was a Christian; he knew God, but he was undecided if he wanted to continue with the marriage.

One day as I was praying, I felt the Holy Spirit tell me, "I am doing a heart transplant on him." His old heart was damaged due to hurt, pain, and trauma, and only God could be the donor and the surgeon for his new heart. Heart transplants take time, and it takes the utmost care to make sure that what is being done is tending to that place of brokenness so that his heart will not fail again.

We prayed that the Holy Spirit would tend to his broken and diseased heart, and that it would begin to beat again not only with a passion for Jesus, but also a passion for his wife and his family. That this heart transplant would be successful and that he could live fully, knowing the love of God, and that any shame he carried would be removed from his old heart. That day, we prayed and asked God to do something supernatural and to complete the heart transformation. We didn't have a quick answer—in fact, as I write this, we are still in the waiting room, waiting for God to do His will in this marriage.

In the waiting room it's hard to hold tight to the promises of God, but that day I prayed that He would give my friend peace, comfort, and joy, knowing that His will would be done in God's perfect timing, regardless of the outcome.

Maybe today you are in the waiting room, waiting for God to do a heart transformation on a loved one. Let me encourage you that God is working—He is working on your behalf, on His timeline. Don't give up and get discouraged; I promise that no matter what the outcome is, His plans are for you and He is still good, even in the midst of the wait.

RESPOND Day 17:

Are you struggling with hurt from the past that is making your heart diseased?

Maybe today you need God to work on your heart— or on the heart of someone you love. Write a letter to God today, telling Him what you need.

Just Breathe

*"I bless God every chance I get; my lungs expand
with his praise. I live and breathe God; if things
aren't going well, hear this and be happy: join me in
spreading the news; together let's get the word out.
God met me more than halfway, he freed me from
my anxious fears"*

(Psalm 34:1-4 MSG)

Have you ever had the wind knocked out of you, or
cried so hard you couldn't catch your breath? It is an incredibly scary feeling not to have breath in your lungs.
When circumstances surround us that take our breath
away, we must rely on Jesus to breathe into us. This isn't
always easy—we want to see the miracle, the outcome—
but often we are in a holding pattern, and it feels like
we're holding our breath. It is often in these times that
we can't even muster up a thank you or find anything
to be grateful for. I have found that gratefulness often
smothers fear. I am not saying that it is easy to be grate-

ful when your world seems to be crumbling around you—in fact, it's one the hardest things that I struggle with.

You see, I am a two on the Enneagram; if you have studied the Enneagram, you may know that I am a helper and a feeler, so when things are not going well I feel all of it, and it often has me spiraling into an emotional abyss. I have had to learn that I can feel those feelings, but only for a time, and then I need to remember all that God has blessed me with and provided for me and be grateful. Gratefulness somehow propels me into joy, anticipation of the good that's coming. I don't want to live in fear and anxiety; when I pour out my praise to Him it frees me to trust God with everything. That means I can be joyful in the midst of every circumstance. Now don't get me wrong—it doesn't mean the sadness goes away; it just means I am making the choice to choose joy in the midst of what I am going through. Finding joy doesn't always mean a smile on your face or a perfect life. Joy is a feeling in your heart that even if your season seems bleak, you can trust that Jesus has you and that He won't let go of you. I challenge you today to take a deep breath, trust Jesus, and choose joy!

RESPOND Day 18:

What are three things you are grateful for today?

Write down three things that were a struggle in your life, but God came through.

Knocked Down but Not Defeated

"Though I fall I will rise; though I dwell in darkness, the LORD is a light for me"

(Micah 7:8 NASB)

I have a confession! Since I was a little girl, I have loved to watch *Rocky* movies. I'm not sure how I got into these movies, but I just remember loving to watch the story of the fighter who was knocked down but always made a triumphant comeback.

When I was thirteen I invited all of my friends over for a slumber party, and these poor girls were subjected to *Rocky 3* at least five times. I'm surprised I still had friends after subjecting them to that!

A few years ago, my husband bought me the whole series—it was honestly one of the best gifts ever! Whenever I go through a tough season, I will often break out the movies and binge-watch them. A few weeks ago,

I busted out the *Rocky 3* movie, and Apollo Creed said something to Rocky after he was defeated by Mr. T. Rocky had walked into a gym full of fighters who were hungry to be the next world champ, and Apollo said, "You see their eyes? That's the eye of the tiger, that edge."

Often in life we lose our edge, our passion. It could just be from the length of our battle, or just that we are prayed out, but that statement caught my ear. *That edge...* That edge to battle, that edge to fight, that edge not to give up. Often in tough seasons we are ready to throw the towel in and give up. God is our edge—He is fighting for us when we get knocked down by the trials of life. We can be secure that the Lion of Judah is behind the scenes, working on our behalf. Did you know that the "eye of the tiger" is a reference to what the tiger's prey sees right before its impending death? When we have the eye of the tiger in our spiritual life, we can be sure that Satan will be defeated. God promised that He will defeat the enemy.

Our situations may look like that final blow: legs wobbly, vision blurred, you can't see anything but darkness. But Jesus promised us that He would be our light. He holds us up when we just can't stand. Today, if you are going through a dark time in your life, I want to encourage you to remember that you have the "eye of the tiger"; that Jesus, our Lion of Judah, has His eye on the prey, and the enemy will be defeated!

RESPOND Day 19:

Have you allowed defeat to keep you from your purpose? If so, why?

Have you lost that "eye of the tiger"? How can you work toward getting your passion back? List three ways to start fulfilling your purpose. They can be simple things; you can start small.

What Fruit Are You Bearing?

*"But the fruit of the Spirit is **love, joy, peace, patience, kindness, goodness, faithfulness, gentleness, self-control;** against such things there is no law. Now those who belong to Christ Jesus have crucified the flesh with its passions and desires"*
(Galatians 5:22-24 NASB)

I walked into the kitchen after a really hard workout and saw this beautiful orange sitting in my fruit bowl. It sounded like the perfect after-workout snack. I grabbed the orange. I could smell the citrus as I peeled the bright orange skin off, and my mouth was watering just thinking about how juicy this orange would be. I took a slice, and to my disappointment it was super dry on the inside, not juicy at all. I was so disappointed! I had such an anticipation of what it was going to be like, and it definitely didn't meet my expectation.

I started to think about the verse about the fruit of the Spirit. If you grew up in church or have been in church for any length of time, you know that this verse is one we have memorized. As I began to ponder that piece of fruit that looked good on the outside but was dry on the inside, I began to wonder if that is how we are.

We seem like we love—we take pictures on our Instagram of us being loving, yet we are actually filled with resentment and hurt.

We say we have peace, yet every day we spend worrying and fretting over things we can't control.

We say we have patience, yet when things take longer than expected we begin to doubt God is listening.

We say we are kind, but the second someone does something we don't like we automatically cut them off or ignore them.

We say we are good, but we often find we are mean and condescending to others.

We say we are faithful, but we forget to spend time with the Lord or dig into His Word, or we are unfaithful to our commitments in our relationships with others.

We say we are gentle, but the second our spouse or kids do something, we react in a harsh way.

We say we have self-control, but we had a bad day, so we decide to binge on food or drinks.

Our flesh gets in the way—and we are human, and that's okay—but it's about our posture on how we react when we see that we aren't living out these fruits. I had a day not too long ago when I was sick and tired of praying and being patient. I literally under my breath was ranting to God, telling Him how angry I was with Him. I went up to my room, reeling with emotion. I jumped into bed, and as I fell asleep, I was still "telling God off." When I woke in the morning, I realized how incredibly ridiculous I was acting. I immediately asked God to forgive me for not trusting Him in the waiting for this prayer request. You see, when we are living out the fruit of the Spirit, even if we fall into our humanness we can get back in line and see that the fruits we are bearing aren't productive in our life. I was reminded that day that I want to continue to practice and be aware of the fruit of the Spirit in my life—to the point that my fruits are not only visible on the outside, but on the inside as well!

So, friends, don't get discouraged if your outside fruit doesn't always match your inside fruit. God is still in the business of redeeming us, even when we fail in our humanness!

RESPOND Day 20:

What fruit do you need to work on most?

Why do you think this fruit is the hardest for you?

Take a few minutes to meditate and pray that God will help you to develop that fruit of the Spirit in your life.

Are You Praying Safe Prayers?

"'What do you want me to do for you?' Jesus asked him. The blind man said, 'Rabbi, I want to see.' 'Go,' said Jesus, 'your faith has healed you.' Immediately he received his sight and followed Jesus along the road"

(Mark 10:51-52 NIV)

I am guilty of only praying prayers that are safe. Can anyone relate? The other day, as I was praying and journaling, I noticed that the prayer in my heart was something I was scared to put down on paper or to even speak out loud. In Mark 10:51, Jesus asks the blind man, "What do you want me to do for you?" Jesus already knew what he needed, but he wanted the man to step out in faith and ask for what he wanted; he wanted his sight back.

As I pondered this scripture, I began to think about things that I wanted—things I was scared to ask for, in case God didn't come through. It was as if, if I asked and He didn't give me what I wanted, God would be shamed. Imagine that—me trying to protect God from the prayers He doesn't answer. I began to see how ridiculous it was to not ask Him. Now if it's God's will, He will do it, and if it is not in His plans, then His plans are greater—but why not ask, why not step out in faith and trust that no matter the outcome, God is in control? I've found that I need to trust God, "even if" my prayers aren't answered in the way I hoped and prayed for. I challenge you to write out your unsafe prayers and see what God will do; it may not be answered in the way you imagined, but your faith will grow.

RESPOND Day 21:

What is a prayer you have that you have been scared to ask for?

If God's answer is different than you were hoping, will you be disappointed?

What holds you back from asking God for the things you want Him to do in your life?

Be Still

"The Lord will fight for you; you need only to be still"
(Exodus 14:14 NIV)

I was watching an old home video with my family the other night, and we were commenting on how much of a busybody our daughter Kalia was. She was always moving and wiggling out of my lap or arms. As much as I would try to keep her still, she would wiggle her way out and run away!

As I began to ponder her movements, I began to think how we are like that with God: we often want to wiggle out of His will for our lives; we want it our way; we want our will to be done, not His will to be done. Maybe you're running away from God because shame is holding you captive, and you think your sin is too big for God to ever love you; or maybe you are in an impossible situation, and you are wondering where God is and if He really is fighting for you.

I have found that it is only when I sit in the stillness with God that He can tend to my heart—to those traumatic, broken places that keep us running or keep us feeling like we aren't enough. God can be trusted with your heart; no matter who has hurt you or who has tried to destroy you, He is your protector and defender, but we must come to Him, sit in His lap, and be still. He wants us to posture our hearts toward Him so that He can heal the brokenness, the betrayal, and the shame in our lives.

God wants to sit with you today; take time to sit and be still and listen to what He is telling you.

RESPOND Day 22:

Why is sitting alone with God hard?

Do you have trouble hearing His voice?

I want you to sit quietly for three minutes, listen to your breath, your heart, and see if you can hear what God is saying to you.

What did you hear? Don't think about it—just write down what you heard the Holy Spirit speak to you.

Sustain

"Cast your burden on the Lord, and he will sustain you; he will never allow the righteous to be shaken"
(Psalm 55:22 CSB)

Let's be real: sustaining is hard. We aren't good at believing that God is sustaining us when we are in the midst of trials. Sustaining means to keep holding on and waiting. I am definitely not an expert at that yet, although I know that I am getting better at it.

I am reminded of the movie *Willy Wonka and the Chocolate Factory*; the ultimate reward wasn't revealed to the children when they entered. Throughout the tour they had all kinds of different journeys, and one by one the kids couldn't abstain from what Willy Wonka told them not to touch or do. Who remembers the character Veruca? She would tell her dad, "I want it now, Daddy," and he would cave in and give it to her. In one particular scene, she wanted the golden chocolate eggs. Willy Wonka tells her she can't have one, and she throws a temper tantrum. She says, "I DON'T CARE HOW; I WANT IT NOW!" She steps on the egg indicator and ends up going down the bad egg shoot! *Poof*—there goes Veruca! She got what she wanted, but it wasn't what she could've had.

That scene always makes me think about how we are with our heavenly Father. We want it now—we don't want to wait, and we don't want to sustain what we are enduring. At the end of the Willy Wonka movie, Charlie ends up getting to own the chocolate factory because he waited, he listened, and he sustained through the whole journey. How often are we like Veruca, or the other kids in the movie—we want it now; we don't want to wait, so we step into something prematurely or make an emotional decision only to have our desires fall short, and then we are disappointed. God promises that if we sustain, He will not allow us to fall or be shaken. God's ways are always better than our ways!

Sustaining is never an easy task; in fact, when we are sustaining it can feel like we can't go on any longer, and we feel like giving up. I encourage you, friends: if you are in a season of sustaining, wait on God. He is working, and when His plans and purposes are revealed, they will be so much greater than what you expected.

RESPOND Day 23:

What does *sustain* mean to you?

When have you waited on God and sustained, and what did it reveal to you?

Has God ever asked you to wait and sustain, and you didn't? What was the outcome?

Forgive and Release

"Get rid of all bitterness, rage and anger, brawling and slander, along with every form of malice. Be kind and compassionate to one another, forgiving each other, just as in Christ God forgave you"
(Ephesians 4:31-32 NIV)

Holding on to things can be detrimental to our growth!

A few years ago, I had a falling out with a friend; we had a heated discussion, and I said something that was hurtful. If I am being honest, so did she, but I knew I needed to step up and ask for forgiveness. I remember standing in front of her, saying, "I am sorry for what I said." She responded back, "Well, I am not sorry for what I said." I was so taken aback; I was apologizing for my part, but she wasn't going to apologize for her part. In that moment I walked away crushed; it wasn't the outcome I expected, and this friendship seemed to be over. I tried multiple times to apologize and even tried to reconcile more than once, but she wasn't having it.

I remember drawing all the curtains in my room and retreating to my bed and crying buckets of tears. I had tried to mend it and I was truly sorry, but the friendship was over. I was devastated. As I cried upstairs, I heard the doorbell ring. It was my friend Phylis; my husband had told her that I was upset, and she immediately came over with French fries and a milkshake in hand. As she walked into the room, I remember her clearly saying, "You did what you could; now you need to release it." That moment was pivotal for me—you see, we can't control others' actions or feelings; we have to do what's right and then release it.

This is something that we need to practice getting good at. If we don't release it, bitterness sets in and personal growth can't happen. Forgiveness isn't about the other person—it's about you releasing it and freeing yourself from the burden of it. I choose to forgive even when it's hard, even when my "I'm sorry" isn't accepted.

Forgiveness is a choice you make. Sometimes it will be received with open arms and restoration of the relationship will happen; other times it won't be received and the relationship will end. But if you choose to forgive and release, it frees you! Remember, the enemy loves division, so this is one of his tactics he uses often.

I think about how we saw so much division in 2020, between the election, racial tensions, and opinions about whether to mask or not to mask. I watched life-long friendships end, and it saddened me that we allowed the enemy to wiggle his way into what we know are the commandments of God. Christ forgave us; He paid the ultimate sacrifice and we continually sin, but He is faithful at forgiving us. So why is it hard for us to forgive? I challenge you, friends: if you are dealing with unforgiveness, ask God to help you. Let Him free you from the bondage that it holds on your life; let go of the resentment and allow freedom to begin!

RESPOND Day 24:

If you struggle with unforgiveness, why is it hard to forgive? Is it past trauma that doesn't allow you to forgive? Was it the way you were raised? Why is forgiveness so hard?

I am going to encourage you to journal here about who you are having a hard time forgiving, releasing them to Jesus.

I pray that as you read this devotional, it encouraged you. We each have a journey in life, and each of our stories are unique. God can use our story to help others, and I hope that you were able to see how God used each disappointment and triumph in my life for His Glory! Don't give up, friends. God sees you, and He is with you!

May God richly bless you and Sparkle on!

Rhonda